Cocktail Book XXL

Master the art of mixing, savoring, and impressing

William Rooley

All advice in this book has been carefully considered and checked by the author and the publisher. However, no guarantee can be given. Any liability of the author or the publisher for any personal injury, property damage or financial loss is therefore excluded.

Cocktail Book XXL

Copyright © 2023 William Rooley

All rights reserved, in particular the right to reproduce and distribute the translation. No part of this work may be reproduced in any form (by photocopy, microfilm or any other process) or stored, processed, duplicated or distributed using electronic systems without the written permission of the publisher.

Circulation 2023

Foreword

Welcome to this cocktail book! Do you enjoy sipping delicious and colorful cocktails with fresh fruits, whether at a trendy bar or on a beautiful beach? Have you ever thought about preparing such exquisite cocktails yourself, whether it's for your partner or friends?

Well, you've come to the right place! In this book, you'll not only learn what makes cocktails special and unique, but you'll also find practical tips on utensils, ingredients, spirits, and everything else a skilled bartender needs to mix and garnish delightful cocktails.

In addition to these insights, this book offers a wide variety of special and diverse recipes. Alongside classics like the Pina Colada, you'll discover unique cocktails that are truly one-of-a-kind. No prior knowledge is required, as anyone can become a pro with the help of this book. Just dive in and start experimenting. Get ready to have a blast mixing your own cocktails—and the best part is that each recipe is accompanied by a photo.

Cheers!

Content

Foreword 3

Introduction to the world of cocktails 9
    What is a cocktail and where does it even come from? 9
    What actually makes a cocktail a cocktail? 10
    What do you need to make the best cocktails yourself? 10

Alcoholic cocktails 11
    Mojito 12
    Red Russian 13
    Mai Tai 14
    Tequila Sunrise 15
    Sour Lemon Aperol 16
    banana cocktail from the Caribbean 17
    cocktail with gin and cucumber 18
    Peach Lemonade Bourbon Cocktail 19
    Exotic Thai Cocktail 20
    egg liqueur cocktail with passion fruit 21
    Cuba Libre 22
    Caipirinha 23
    cocktail with RosÉ mulled wine 24
    Tropical Colada 25
    strawberry colada 26
    Green Gin 27
    Wonderful colorful cocktail 28
    lime cocktail with coconut milk 29
    Creamy white Russian 30
    Black Panther with lemonade 31
    Strawberry Margarita 32
    Hot apple amaretto 33
    Aperol Lemonade 34

Purple Sky	*35*
Forever Blue Friends Cocktail	*36*
Sparkling New Year's Eve Cocktail	*37*
Ginger Sunrise	*38*
mulled lillet with raspberries	*39*
Aperol punch with rose water	*40*
Pina Colada	*41*
blueberry mojito	*42*
Dark Orange Cocktail	*43*
Sweet Red Lady Cocktail	*44*
Fruity Pink Easter Cocktail	*45*
banana pancake cocktail	*46*
Cocktail with banana and peanut butter	*47*
Creamy Moose Milk Cocktail	*48*
Italian Liquid Tiramisu	*49*
Green cocktail with fresh kiwi	*50*
Refreshing peach cocktail with sage	*51*
Aromatic sweet hurricane cocktail	*52*
Aperol Caipi Cocktail	*53*
Christmas Cranberry Gin and Tonic	*54*
Hawaiian Maui Mule	*55*
Winter Blueberry Cinnamon Cocktail	*56*
Christmas Cinnamon Orange Cocktail	*57*
Heavenly snow punch	*58*
Red Pomegranate Mule	*59*
Hot Cranberry Punch	*60*
Hot Berry Punch	*61*
Christmas orange punch with rum	*62*
Delicious Halloween Cocktail	*63*
Fruity cocktail with pomegranate and mint	*64*
Blue Swimming Pool Cocktail	*65*
Yellow Slushie Cocktail	*66*
Pink Lady Cocktail	*67*
Heavenly Malibu Sunset Cocktail	*68*

Pink coconut cocktail......69
Summer watermelon cocktail......70
Purple Caipirinha......71
Berry Cardamom Bramble......72
Creamy milk cocktail with rum and honey......73
Spicy Ginger Gin Cocktail......74
Dream eggnog......75
Exotic Blue Sparkling Wine Cocktail......76

Cocktails without alcohol......77

Colourful rainbow cocktail......78
Delicious Ipanema......79
Refreshing Nojito (Mojito without alcohol)......80
Invigorating Hugo......81
Sparkling mojito with fresh mango......82
Autumn Rosehip Cocktail......83
Tropical cocktail with fresh pineapple......84
Woodruff cocktail for children......85
Fruity Multi Colada......86
Mango cocktail with elderberry......87
Sweet mango ginger cocktail......88
Colored cocktail with kiwi......89
Chai Bubble Tea Latte......90
Booster cocktail with rosehip......91
Delicious berry cocktail......92
High Protein Smoothie Cocktail......93
Blueberry Banana Cocktail......94
Green Smoothie Cocktail......95
Simple strawberry cocktail......96
Delicious strawberry cocktail with tangerine......97
Aromatic Hugo punch with strawberries......98
Hawaiian Lava Flow Cocktail......99
Apple cocktail with cranberry juice......100
Happy cocktail with passion fruit......101

Refreshing soda cocktail for summer	102
Sweet cocktail with lime	103
Fruity Mango Lassi Cocktail	104
Pink Blueberry Lemonade Cocktail	105
Thirst quenching Crodino Ginger Tonic	106
Mango cocktail with fresh mint	107
Colourful fruit punch	108
Coconut Yogurt Cocktail	109
New Year's Eve cocktail with strawberry juice	110
Apple Cherry Tonic	111
Gaudy Primavera	112
Delicious pear cocktail	113
Vitamin cocktail with sea buckthorn	114
Bora Bora Cocktail	115
Fruity and creamy gin cocktail	116
Raspberry punch with fresh rosemary	117
Exotic swimming pool	118
Invigorating cocktail with coffee	119
Bittersweet cocktail with mint	120
Dark Energy Cocktail	121
Delicious Pelican Cocktail	122
Creamy apple punch with cream	123
Iced cocktail with cherries and pineapple	124
Delicious passion fruit mango cocktail	125
White Blueberry Cocktail	126
Fruity Lemonade Cocktail with Pomegranate	127
Juicy Banana Cocktail	128
Strawberry Garden Cocktail	129
Valentine's Day cocktail with elderberry	130
pomegranate cocktail	131
Invigorating peach rosé	132
Refreshing Watermelon Gin Tonic	133
Creamy orange pineapple cocktail	134
Delicious orange punch	135

Introduction to the world of cocktails

WHAT IS A COCKTAIL AND WHERE DOES IT EVEN COME FROM?

Refreshing and often alcoholic mixed drinks are typically prepared with care and precision, skillfully mixed in a shaker. The result is then lovingly arranged in a suitable glass and served immediately. Each cocktail is unique and often bears a distinctive name, some of which have gained international recognition.

The word "cocktail" has a fascinating history that dates back to the 19th century. It was first used to describe a invigorating beverage consisting of a harmonious blend of sugar, spirits, and water. Even back then, cocktails were often enhanced with fresh herbs to add an aromatic touch. The term itself originated in the English-speaking world and has since become established in the realm of mixed drinks.

WHAT ACTUALLY MAKES A COCKTAIL A COCKTAIL?

A cocktail distinguishes itself from a regular long drink by consisting of at least three ingredients. In contrast, a long drink typically comprises just two ingredients, with an alcoholic beverage being topped up with a non-alcoholic one. However, what makes a cocktail truly special is its preparation: it is shaken, not simply poured into the glass. Additionally, cocktails are often served in beautiful glasses adorned with decorative elements to complete the overall experience.

It's worth mentioning that non-alcoholic cocktails are referred to as mocktails, providing a delightful alternative for those who prefer to abstain from alcohol.

WHAT DO YOU NEED TO MAKE THE BEST COCKTAILS YOURSELF?

To prepare alcoholic cocktails, various spirits are naturally required. It is recommended to have the following types of spirits on hand: white rum, dark rum, gin, bourbon, brandy, vodka, or tequila. These spirits are among the most commonly used in the art of mixology. For best results, using a cocktail shaker is advised, as a cocktail is ideally shaken. Alternatively, a conventional mixer can be used, but a true professional swears by a shaker.

Most cocktails also call for fresh lemon or lime juice, so it's useful to have a high-quality citrus press available. Other useful utensils include a mixing glass, a jigger, a strainer, ice cube molds, and a muddler. To prepare fresh cocktails, always have fresh fruit, fresh herbs, mixers (such as mineral water or ginger ale), simple syrup, and ice or crushed ice on hand. With these essentials, nothing will stand in the way of your mixing adventure.

Alcoholic cocktails

MOJITO

Ingredients for 1 jar:

5 cl white rum
6 cl soda to top up
1 lime
4 tbsp crushed ice
2 tsp brown sugar
8 leaves of fresh mint

Preparation:

1. First wash the lime and cut off the ends. Then cut the lime into eight pieces and put them in a suitable glass together with the cane sugar. Then add the mint.

2. Now mash the lime and the mint so that a little juice comes out. The lime should not be crushed!

3. Fill the glass with the crushed ice. Then add the white rum and fill up the rest with water.

4. Garnish the finished mojito with lime slices or some mint, if desired.

RED RUSSIAN

Ingredients:
4 cl vodka
25 ml cherry liqueur
3 small ice cubes
1 sprig of fresh mint
1 cocktail cherry

Preparation:
1. Put the small ice cubes in a glass and then add the cherry liqueur.

2. Pour vodka and mix a little.

3. Put a cocktail cherry in the glass and garnish with a little fresh mint.

MAI TAI

Ingredients for 1 jar:

6 cl white or brown rum
2 cl Cointreau
1 cl lime juice
1 cl sugar syrup
1 cl almond syrup
1 lime
Ice cubes or crushed ice

Preparation:

1. Crush a few ice cubes or use crushed ice and pour it into a glass.

2. Cut the lime into quarters and squeeze over the glass. Then add the squeezed quarters to the ice in the glass.

3. Take a cocktail shaker, pour in all the other ingredients and shake vigorously.

4. Pour the finished cocktail into the glass with the ice and garnish as desired.

TEQUILA SUNRISE

Ingredients for 1 jar:

4 cl tequila
15 cl orange juice
1 cl grenadine
Ice cubes or crushed ice

Preparation:

1. Put a few ice cubes or some crushed ice in your glass.

2. Pour in the tequila and orange juice.

3. Carefully run the grenadine around the rim of the glass with a teaspoon and then stir calmly with a small stick - this creates a beautiful sunrise colour.

4. Garnish if desired and enjoy immediately.

SOUR LEMON APEROL

Ingredients for 1 jar:
4 cl gin
4 cl Aperol
2 cl lemon juice (from one fresh lemon)
2 tsp white sugar
Some ice cubes

Preparation:
1. Pour all ingredients into a shaker and shake vigorously.

2. The finished cocktail is best served in whiskey glasses.

3. Decorate the cold drink with delicious slices of lemon.

BANANA COCKTAIL FROM THE CARIBBEAN

Ingredients for 1 jar:

½ a banana
A handful of ice-cream
4 cl coconut milk
3 cl pineapple juice
1 cl grenadine
4 cl white rum
Pineapple and banana for garnish

Preparation:

1. Get a blender ready. First pour in the coconut milk, pineapple juice, grenadine and white rum.

2. Add the half chopped banana, then mix everything thoroughly.

3. Fill the ice in a glass and pour the mixed cocktail over it.

4. If desired, you can put small pieces of pineapple and banana slices on a skewer to decorate the cocktail.

COCKTAIL WITH GIN AND CUCUMBER

Ingredients for 1 jar:

A small piece of cucumber
4 cl gin
1 cl sugar syrup
2 cl St. Germain elderflower syrup
2 cl lemon juice
4 cl apple juice
Some ice cubes

Preparation:

1. It is best to use a cocktail shaker. Add the cucumber, sugar syrup and lemon juice. Now mix everything vigorously.

2. Add the remaining ingredients and shake everything again vigorously.

3. Pour the finished drink into a larger glass. Then decorate the cocktail with a few fresh cucumber slices.

PEACH LEMONADE BOURBON COCKTAIL

Ingredients for 1 jar:

½ a ripe peach
4 cl bourbon
A handful of ice-cream
12 cl Italian lemonade or mineral water
Peach wedges for decoration

Preparation:

1. Cut the peach into small pieces and puree them very finely with a blender.

2. Pour the peach puree into a glass and mix with bourbon. Stir.

3. Add the ice to the glass and then fill the glass with Italian lemonade.

EXOTIC THAI COCKTAIL

Ingredients for 2 drinks:

2 passion fruits
8 cl vodka
250 ml mango juice
2 tsp Maille mustard mango and Thai seasoning
Some ice cubes
100 ml mineral water

Preparation:

1. First halve the passion fruits and scrape out the pulps with a spoon.

2. Put the pulp in a cocktail shaker together with the vodka, juice and mustard.

3. Add more ice to the shaker, then close it and shake it properly for 10 seconds.

4. Add a few ice cubes to the glasses and pour the cocktail through a sieve into the glasses. Add the mineral water to the cocktail and stir once. Garnish with exotic fruit pieces as desired.

EGG LIQUEUR COCKTAIL WITH PASSION FRUIT

Ingredients for 1 jar:

5 cl eggnog
2 cl white rum
8 cl passion fruit juice
2 cl passion fruit syrup
12 tbsp crushed ice
½ an orange peel

Preparation:

1. First add the eggnog, white rum, passion fruit syrup and juice to a shaker. Add the crushed ice and shake well.

2. Pour the mixture through a sieve into a large glass and fill it with 6 tbsp of crushed ice.

3. Finally, decorate with half an orange slice.

CUBA LIBRE

Ingredients for 1 jar:
4 cl white rum
15 cl cola
½ a lime

Preparation:
1. Wash the lime and then cut it into quarters. Squeeze a little over the glass and then add to the glass.

2. Pour the rum over the lime and top up the cocktail with the cola. If desired, add some crushed ice or a few ice cubes to make the cocktail even more refreshing.

CAIPIRINHA

Ingredients for 1 jar:

6 cl cachaca
2 tsp brown cane sugar
1 lime
Some lime juice if desired

Preparation:

1. Cut the lime into quarters. Then squeeze a little juice from the limes into the glass.

2. Put the lime pieces into the glass and add the sugar. Then mix with a stick. Fill up the glass with the cachaca and add ice to the glass until it is full. Now stir everything together again.

3. If the limes have not yet released enough juice, you can add more lime juice.

COCKTAIL WITH ROSÉ MULLED WINE

Ingredients for 1 jar:
1 bottle of rosé wine
2 - 3 tbsp brown sugar
½ an apple
2 sticks of cinnamon
1 vanilla pod
1 star anise

Preparation:
1. Put the wine in a saucepan and heat it over medium heat.

2. Cut the apple into slices about 1 cm thick.

3. Take a star-shaped cookie and cut out stars from the apple.

4. Add the stars to the wine in the pot.

5. Now cut open the vanilla pod. Add the star anise, cinnamon and the vanilla pod to the wine.

6. Depending on the desired sweetness, add 2 - 3 tbsp of brown rock candy. If the wine is sweet, you will need a little less sugar.

7. The mulled wine should not boil, because the alcohol will evaporate and the spices can become bitter.

8. Let the wine steep a little longer.

TROPICAL COLADA

Ingredients for 4 drinks:

40 ml Myers Rum
30 ml Grand Marnier (orange liqueur)
30 ml Batida de Coco (coconut liqueur)
70 ml canned coconut cream
80 ml whipped cream
50 ml unsweetened pomegranate juice
15 ml passion fruit juice
15 ml pineapple juice
Crushed ice
Fresh pineapple and strawberries to garnish

Preparation:

1. Add all ingredients, except for the fresh fruit, into a stand mixer or shaker. Mix everything well for a few seconds.

2. Now fill four glasses with crushed ice. Add everything to the cocktail and decorate with fresh pineapple and strawberries.

STRAWBERRY COLADA

Ingredients for 4 drinks:

250 g strawberries
240 ml coconut milk
120 g cream
320 ml pineapple juice
200 ml white rum
2 handfuls of crushed ice

Preparation:

1. Thoroughly wash the strawberries. Remove the green and save about 4 strawberries for decoration.

2. Put the other strawberries in a tall container and puree them very finely with a blender.

3. Distribute half of the crushed ice among the cocktail glasses.

4. Place the other half in a shaker with the coconut milk, rum, cream and pineapple juice. Then shake thoroughly for about 20 seconds.

5. Pour the finished cocktail into glasses and then carefully slide the strawberry puree into them, stirring it in a bit to create a nice gradient.

6. Decorate each glass with a strawberry and serve immediately.

GREEN GIN

Ingredients for 2 drinks:
½ a bunch of celery
2 cucumbers
2 lemons
4 cl gin
250 ml soda water for infusion
Some ice-cream as desired

Preparation:
1. First wash the celery and remove the stalks.

2. Wash the cucumber and cut off the ends. Then halve the cucumber and cut lengthwise into quarters. Put 4 stalks to the side for decoration.

3. Put the celery and cucumber in a juicer.

4. Cut the lemons in half and squeeze them. Now mix the lemon juice with the juice and decant into two large glasses.

5. Add 2 cl gin each and fill up with soda. Garnish with the cucumbers if desired and add some ice.

WONDERFUL COLORFUL COCKTAIL

Ingredients for 1 jar:

1 cl Blue Curacao
3 cl cachaca
2 cl Batida de Coco
1 cl banana syrup
6 cl orange juice
5 cl passion fruit juice

Preparation:

1. Pour all ingredients except the Blue Curacao into a shaker. Add ice cubes and shake everything vigorously.

2. Pour the drink through a sieve and into a highball glass. Add ice cubes if desired.

3. Carefully add the Blue Curacao with a small spoon. Serve the cocktail with a straw and garnish with fresh exotic fruits as desired.

LIME COCKTAIL WITH COCONUT MILK

Ingredients for 1 jar:
8 cl fresh coconut milk
4 cl Cointreau
1 cl fresh lime juice
Some ice cubes
Some crushed ice

Preparation:
1. Pour the coconut milk, 4 cl Cointreau and the fresh juice into a shaker. Add the ice cubes and shake everything well.

2. Now pour through a fine sieve and into a glass filled with crushed ice.

CREAMY WHITE RUSSIAN

Ingredients for 1 jar:

4 cl vodka
2 cl coffee liqueur
1 cl cream
Some ice cubes

Preparation:

1. Fill a large glass with ice cubes. Then add coffee liqueur and vodka.

2. Pour the cream into a bowl and whip.

3. Simply fill the glass with the cream.

BLACK PANTHER WITH LEMONADE

Ingredients for 1 jar:
2 cl grenadine syrup
Some pink hail sugar
1 dragon fruit
55 ml grenadine syrup
4 cl black vodka
2 cl Blue Curacao liqueur
100 ml lemonade
4 cl lime juice
Some ice cubes

Preparation:
1. Fill a shallow plate with a tbsp of grenadine. Then dip the rims of the cocktail glasses and roll them in the hail sugar on another plate. Let the glass dry.

2. Halve the dragon fruit and cut out balls with a small spoon. Put them to the side.

3. For the cocktail, add all liquid ingredients together with the ice cubes in a shaker and shake well.

4. Pour the mixed drink into the prepared glasses and serve together with scoops of dragon fruit.

STRAWBERRY MARGARITA

Ingredients for 1 jar:

2 cl Cointreau
2 cl tequila
2 cl lemon juice
4 cl strawberry syrup
6 fresh or frozen strawberries
Crushed ice or ice cubes

Preparation:

1. Blend all of the ingredients in a blender until the strawberries are nice and fine.

2. Now use a cocktail shaker. Pour in crushed ice and the mixed ingredients. Shake well again.

3. Pour the finished cocktail into a large glass and serve immediately. If you like, you can decorate the glass with strawberries or put them on a stick.

HOT APPLE AMARETTO

Ingredients for 1 jar:
200 ml apple juice
150 ml amaretto
200 ml cream
Some cinnamon

Preparation:
1. Pour the whipped cream into a bowl and whip until stiff. Then place it in a piping bag.

2. Put the apple juice and the amaretto into a saucepan and heat - do not bring to a boil!

3. Pour the apple-amaretto mixture into a large glass.

4. Now add the cream with the piping bag and sprinkle the drink with cinnamon. Before drinking, mix in the cream a little.

APEROL LEMONADE

Ingredients for 1 jar:
60 ml Aperol
20 ml hibiscus syrup
20 ml lemon juice
Mineral water
A few slices of lemon
A few ice cubes or crushed ice

Preparation:

1. Put the Aperol, lemon juice, hibiscus syrup and a few ice cubes in a glass.

2. Fill the glass with water.

3. Decorate the delicious drink with freshly cut lemon slices.

PURPLE SKY

Ingredients for 1 jar:

For the sugar rim on the glass:

30 g sugar
Purple food colouring
1 tsp water

For the cocktail:

40 g vodka
10 g amaretto
50 g whole milk yoghurt
20 g cream
40 g milk
1 tsp vanilla syrup
A squeeze of fresh lemon juice
6 ice cubes
Purple food colouring

Preparation:

1. First, mix the sugar with the food colouring and water in a small bowl.

2. Hold the glass upside down and run a lemon slice over the rim. Then press the moistened rim into the coloured sugar mixture.

3. For the cocktail, add all ingredients to a shaker. Then mix thoroughly for 20 - 30 seconds.

4. Pour the finished cocktail into the prepared glass and serve the Purple Sky with a straw.

FOREVER BLUE FRIENDS COCKTAIL

Ingredients for 1 jar:
4 ice cubes
1 cl Blue Curacao
5 cl gin
Tonic water
1 lemon

Preparation:

1. First, fill a large glass with a few ice cubes. Then pour 1 cl Blue Curacao over it.

2. Pour the gin, stir everything briefly and fill with the tonic water.

3. Cut a thick slice of lemon and stick it on the rim of the glass. Then decorate the cocktail with a colourful straw.

SPARKLING NEW YEAR'S EVE COCKTAIL

Ingredients for 2 drinks:
Juice of one lemon
2 tbsp sugar for the rims of the glasses
50 ml white rum
50 ml Curacao Blue
Crushed ice
200 ml pineapple juice
200 ml dry sparkling wine
A few cocktail cherries
Fresh mint

Preparation:
1. Put the sugar and lemon juice on separate small plates.

2. Dip the rims of the glasses in the juice and then immediately in the sugar.

3. Decorate the rims of the glasses with some mint and cocktail cherries.

4. Now mix the rum and curacao.

5. Add the crushed ice. Finally, fill the glasses with pineapple juice and sparkling wine.

GINGER SUNRISE

Ingredients for 10 drinks:

600 ml orange juice
600 ml pineapple juice
300 ml coconut rum
600 ml ginger ale
300 ml grenadine syrup

Preparation:

1. First, put the orange juice, pineapple juice and ginger ale in a shaker and shake well. Then add the rum and mix well again.

2. Divide the finished cocktail among the glasses and spoon the syrup into the glasses in a thin stream - 30 ml each, depending on the sweetness. The syrup should then settle at the bottom.

Small tip: Fruit skewers taste wonderfully with it.

MULLED LILLET WITH RASPBERRIES

Ingredients for 2 drinks:

400 g water
3 tea bags of raspberry tea
50 g raspberry syrup
100 g Lillet
Fresh or frozen raspberries

Preparation:

1. For better taste, you can soak the raspberries in Lillet a day before.

2. Boil the water in a kettle.

3. Put the raspberry flavoured tea bags in the water and let them brew for about 5 minutes.

4. Add the raspberry syrup to the tea. After that, add the Lillet.

5. More syrup or Lillet can be added to taste.

6. Pour the finished drink into two cups and add the fresh or thawed raspberries.

APEROL PUNCH WITH ROSE WATER

Ingredients for approx. 2 L punch:

10 untreated roses
5 tbsp Aperol
1 L sweet white wine
2 tbsp rose water
0,7 L dry sparkling wine

Preparation:

1. It is best to use a nice big bowl for the punch.

2. In the bowl, mix the Aperol, the white wine and the rose water.

3. Remove the rose petals from the stems and add them to the punch.

4. Let the drink stand for at least two hours so that it infuses well.

5. If desired, you can add a little more rose water.

6. Top up the punch with the sparkling wine shortly before serving. Add ice if desired to make the punch even more refreshing.

PINA COLADA

Ingredients for 1 jar:

6 cl white rum
10 cl pineapple juice
4 cl thick coconut cream (Cream of Coconut)
2 cl whipped cream
3 - 4 ice cubes
1 pineapple slice
1 cocktail cherry

Preparation:

1. First fill the rum in a container for mixing.

2. Add the pineapple juice, coconut cream and cream and mix vigorously.

3. Pour into a larger cocktail glass and garnish with a pineapple slice and cocktail cherry. Enjoy chilled.

BLUEBERRY MOJITO

Ingredients for 2 drinks:

20 g blueberries
4 tbsp brown cane sugar
2 cl lime juice
8 cl rum
2 stalks of fresh mint
0,5 L tonic water
Crushed ice
4 cl Blue Curacao

Preparation:

1. Wash the blueberries and crush half of them roughly with the sugar.

2. Mix the crushed blueberries with the lime juice and rum. Divide the mixture between two glasses.

3. Now wash the mint and put into the glasses. Then fill the glasses with tonic water and crushed ice.

4. Carefully run the Blue Curacao over a teaspoon around the rims into the glasses.

DARK ORANGE COCKTAIL

Ingredients for 2 drinks:

200 ml grapefruit lemonade
4 cl orange liqueur
2 dashes of Angostura
2 cl freshly squeezed lemon juice
4 sprigs of fresh thyme
Some ice cubes
1 bottle of Imperial Stout
A few slices of orange
A few sprigs of fresh thyme
4 - 6 ice cubes

Preparation:

1. Pour the lemonade, orange liqueur, Angostura and fresh lemon juice into a tall container.

2. Pluck the thyme leaves from the sprig and add them. Add as many ice cubes as you like and stir everything thoroughly.

3. Now add a few ice cubes to the glasses and divide the lemonade mixture between the glasses.

4. Garnish both glasses with some thyme and fresh orange slices.

SWEET RED LADY COCKTAIL

Ingredients for 1 jar:

40 ml gin
20 ml raspberry or grenadine syrup
40 ml still water
20 ml lemon juice
Crushed ice
1 short black straw

Preparation:

1. Fill the glass with crushed ice until it is completely full.

2. Pour the gin, fresh lemon juice and still water into a wine glass.

3. Add the sweet raspberry syrup to the glass.

4. Finally, stir all the ingredients with a straw. Afterwards, the cocktail can be garnished and enjoyed as desired.

FRUITY PINK EASTER COCKTAIL

Ingredients for 8 drinks:
1 bottle of lemonade (0,75 L)
50 ml strawberry syrup
80 - 160 ml gin
Ice cubes
Edible flowers for garnishing

Preparation:
1. First mix the lemonade with the strawberry syrup.

2. Place the ice cubes into 8 champagne glasses and then add about 10 - 20 ml of gin.

3. Now pour the lemonade into the glasses and garnish the finished cocktail with edible flowers or even a few rose petals.

BANANA PANCAKE COCKTAIL

Ingredients for 1 jar:
6 cl Plantation Rum
½ a banana
Some honey
Juice of one lime
0,5 cl Orgeat
0,5 cl chocolate liqueur
Fresh mint for garnish
Fresh banana slices for garnish

Preparation:
1. First fry the banana in a little oil.

2. Put the lime in a pan and roast it a little.

3. Mix the banana with a little honey, then let caramelize.

4. Put the banana and the juice of the roasted lime into a shaker and shake well.

5. Add the rum and 0.5 cl Orgeat. Add more ice and shake everything vigorously again.

6. Fill ice in a nice glass and pour the cocktail. Stir once briefly.

7. Now slowly add the chocolate liqueur to the glass.

8. Garnish the finished drink with mint and banana slices.

COCKTAIL WITH BANANA AND PEANUT BUTTER

Ingredients for 1 jar:
4,5 cl Irish Whiskey
4,5 cl Irish Cream
1 tbsp peanut butter
1 banana
4 tbsp vanilla ice cream

Preparation:
1. First put the ice cream and the remaining ingredients into a blender or grind them with a blender until fine.

2. Pour the mixture into a glass and garnish the cocktail with fresh banana slices or with some chocolate, if desired.

3. Little tip: spooning the cocktail is best.

CREAMY MOOSE MILK COCKTAIL

Ingredients for 1 jar:

4 cl dark rum
2 cl Bourbon whiskey
2 cl coffee liqueur
3 cl maple syrup
20 cl fresh whole milk
2 thick spoonfuls of vanilla ice cream

Preparation:

1. First pour the alcohol in a blender and mix everything briefly.

2. Add the remaining ingredients and blend until creamy.

3. Now pour the mixture into a glass, garnish with a little nutmeg and serve with a spoon.

ITALIAN LIQUID TIRAMISU

Ingredients for 1 jar:
2 cl espresso
1 cl amaretto
2 cl dark chocolate liqueur
2 cl dark rum

Preparation:
1. First, pour the freshly made espresso into a glass using the back of a spoon.

2. Also with a spoon, add the amaretto to the glass.

3. Add the rum and liqueur. In the end, there should be nice layers in the glass.

4. It's best to garnish the cocktail with some cocoa powder and a small cookie.

GREEN COCKTAIL WITH FRESH KIWI

Ingredients for 1 jar:

5 cl gin
1 kiwi
18 tarragon leaves
2,5 cl fresh lime juice
1,5 cl sugar syrup
Cold mineral water
Ice

Preparation:

1. Peel the fresh kiwi and cut it into slices.

2. Put them in a shaker with the tarragon and shake well.

3. Add the gin, fresh lime juice and sugar syrup to a shaker.

4. Add some more ice and mix again vigorously for several seconds.

5. Fill a large glass with ice cubes and pour in the cocktail. Pour in the mineral water and then decorate it with fresh tarragon.

REFRESHING PEACH COCKTAIL WITH SAGE

Ingredients for 4 drinks:
200 ml Pimm's No.1
400 ml ginger ale
1 untreated lemon
2 fresh peaches
½ a cucumber
4 fresh sprigs of sage
Some ice cubes

Preparation:
1. First fill four glasses with ice cubes.

2. Wash the lemon and cut into slices. Wash the cucumber and cut it into thin sticks. Divide both between the glasses.

3. Top up each glass with 50 ml of Pimm's and 100 ml of ginger ale.

4. Garnish the finished cocktails with fresh sage.

AROMATIC SWEET HURRICANE COCKTAIL

Ingredients for 1 jar:

5 cl white rum
5 cl dark rum
5 cl passion fruit juice
2,5 cl orange juice
2 cl lime juice
1 tbsp sugar syrup
1 tbsp grenadine

Preparation:

1. Gradually add the ingredients to a blender or cocktail shaker.

2. Mix the ingredients vigorously for about 20 seconds.

3. Pour into a suitable glass and garnish with fresh fruit as desired.

APEROL CAIPI COCKTAIL

Ingredients for 1 jar:

6 cl Aperol
1 tsp brown cane sugar
A fresh lime
A few ice cubes or crushed ice

Preparation:

1. Cut the lime into small pieces and put them in a large glass.

2. Add the brown sugar and mash the limes a little with a chopstick.

3. Add the Aperol and fill the glass with ice cubes or crushed ice.

4. If desired, you can top up the Aperol with mineral water. Garnish the finished cocktail with fresh strawberries.

CHRISTMAS CRANBERRY GIN AND TONIC

Ingredients for 1 jar:

1 tbsp sugar
4 cl gin
8 cl cranberry juice
80 ml tonic water
Some ice cubes
3 - 4 fresh cranberries
5 cm cucumber

Preparation:

1. First decorate the glass a little. To do this, simply sprinkle a little sugar on a small plate. Then moisten the rim of the glass with water.

2. Turn the rim of the glass slowly through the sugar so that it sticks. The rim should look like snow and taste great.

3. Take the cucumber slice and cut out a fir tree with a mould or cut out a fir tree freehand with a knife. Put the tree on a skewer for decoration.

4. For the cocktail, pour the gin and the cranberry juice into the glass and mix. First fill up the glass with tonic water.

5. Add the fresh cranberries and a few ice cubes.

HAWAIIAN MAUI MULE

Ingredients for 1 jar:
1 tea bag of butterfly pea flower tea
300 ml water
4 cl berry vodka liqueur
2 cl vodka
2 cl lime juice
50 ml passion fruit juice
100 ml ginger beer
6 tbsp crushed ice

Preparation:
1. Fill water into a large glass and add the tea bag. Steep for about 10 minutes until the water has turned a deep blue colour.

2. Pour the water into ramekins to make ice cubes. Freeze and later turn into crushed ice.

3. Now add the alcohol, passion fruit juice and fresh lime juice to a shaker. Also add 2 tbsp of the blue crushed ice. Then shake everything thoroughly for a few seconds.

4. Pour the rest of the crushed ice into the glass. Then pour the contents of the shaker through a sieve into the glass.

5. Infuse with ginger beer.

WINTER BLUEBERRY CINNAMON COCKTAIL

Ingredients for 1 jar:

3 cl Bourbon whiskey
3 cl blueberry juice from frozen blueberries
2 cl cinnamon syrup (e.g. monin)
3 dashes of Angostura bitter
Sparkling mineral water
Some fresh lime juice as needed
1 cinnamon stick
A sprig of fresh rosemary
A few frozen blueberries
Ice cubes or crushed ice

Preparation:

1. First make the fresh blueberry juice. To do this, let the blueberries thaw and then pass them through a very fine sieve. Collect the juice. Bought blueberry juice is in most cases too sweet for the recipe.

2. Now put the ice cubes in a large glass. Then add the whiskey, blueberry juice, cinnamon syrup and Angostura bitter. Stir everything once. Fill up the cocktail with cold mineral water. If the mixture is too sweet, you can add some lime juice.

3. Garnish the finished cocktail with a cinnamon stick and fresh rosemary - of course you can use other items.

4. Finally, add a few frozen blueberries and then the wintry cocktail can be drunk immediately.

CHRISTMAS CINNAMON ORANGE COCKTAIL

Ingredients for 4 drinks:

1 L freshly squeezed orange juice
2 tbsp honey
2 tsp cinnamon
½ tsp gingerbread spice
A little sugar to taste
Some sugar for decoration
A dash of vodka
A few fresh cranberries
1 lemon

Preparation:

1. First squeeze the juice of several oranges until you have about 1 L of juice.

2. Pour the juice into a large pot and heat it slowly. Do not bring the juice to a boil, otherwise vitamins may be lost.

3. Now add the honey, cinnamon and gingerbread spice. Add the vodka and season.

4. For sweetness, you can mix in a little more sugar.

5. Cut the fresh lemon and drag it along the edge of your glass. After, dip the rim in some sugar. Let everything dry.

6. Afterwards, put fresh cranberries on a wooden skewer and insert it into the winter drink for decoration.

HEAVENLY SNOW PUNCH

Ingredients for 1 jar:
2 cl brown rum
1 cinnamon stick
250 ml milk
100 ml cream
1 pinch of cinnamon
1 tbsp brown sugar

Preparation:
1. First heat 250 ml of milk in a small saucepan. Then add the sugar and stir a little. After it has dissolved, whisk the milk.

2. Pour the heated milk into a glass and mix in the brown rum.

3. Now whip the cream in a bowl until stiff and put it on top of the punch.

4. Garnish with a cinnamon stick and dust the cream with ground cinnamon.

RED POMEGRANATE MULE

Ingredients for 2 drinks:

4 cl vodka
1 pinch of cinnamon
100 ml apple juice
200 ml pomegranate juice
Some Thomas Henry Spicy Ginger Beer for infusion
A few pomegranate seeds
4 thinly sliced apples
Ice cream

Preparation:

1. Fill each glass with 2 cl vodka and add the pomegranate seeds and ice cubes.

2. Sprinkle with a pinch of cinnamon and add the apple juice and pomegranate juice. Stir once.

3. Add the Spicy Ginger Beer and garnish with pomegranate seeds and fresh apple slices if desired.

HOT CRANBERRY PUNCH

Ingredients for 6 drinks:

1 bottle of Merlot (Cabernet Sauvignon or Zinfandel)
200 ml orange juice
300 ml cranberry juice
65 g sugar
1 untreated orange
2 cloves
2 cinnamon sticks
120 ml brandy

Preparation:

1. First put the red wine, cranberry juice, orange juice and sugar in a pot.

2. Wash the orange and sprinkle with cloves.

3. Add the orange and the cinnamon sticks to the pot and let everything simmer for about 1.5 hours.

4. Remove the orange and cinnamon sticks and pour the hot punch through a sieve into a large bowl.

5. Pour the punch back into the pot and add the brandy. Add sugar to taste.

6. Pour the finished punch into glasses and garnish with fresh fruit or cinnamon sticks.

HOT BERRY PUNCH

Ingredients for 1 jar:

100 ml aronia juice
80 ml blackcurrant juice
120 ml cranberry juice
6 cl rum
1 cinnamon stick
1 star anise
4 cloves
½ an orange
3 tbsp trail mix

Preparation:

1. Pour all the juices together in a pot and heat them.

2. Add the spices and leave to infuse for about 15 minutes.

3. Now pour the trail mix into 2 cups and fill each with 3 cl rum.

4. Peel half of the orange and add the unpeeled half to the pot.

5. Cut the other half into wedges and place into the cups.

6. Distribute the contents from the pot into the cups.

CHRISTMAS ORANGE PUNCH WITH RUM

Ingredients for 2 drinks:
250 ml black tea
4 oranges
4 tbsp white rum
1 pinch of cinnamon
¼ vanilla pod
1 cardamom pod
Candy as required

Preparation:
1. First squeeze the juice out of the oranges.

2. Warm the tea together with the orange juice in a pot.

3. Now scrape out the pith of the vanilla and add to the oranges with the cinnamon, rum and cardamom.

4. Serve the hot punch in glasses or cups and add more sweetener as needed.

DELICIOUS HALLOWEEN COCKTAIL

Ingredients for 4 drinks:

4 tbsp sugar
Black food colouring
50 ml vodka
100 ml Blue Curacao
150 ml cranberry juice
50 ml grenadine syrup
75 ml sweet and sour syrup
Ice cream

Preparation:

1. Rub the sugar and the food between your hands so that the colour mixes well with the sugar. It is best to wear gloves when doing this.

2. Now mix the vodka, Blue Curacao, cranberry juice, grenadine and 50 ml of grenadine syrup.

3. Then, place 3 - 4 tablespoons of sweet and sour syrup on a small plate. Spread the grey sugar on a different plate.

4. Stick the rim of the glasses first into the syrup and then directly into the sugar - this forms a nice rim.

5. Fill the glasses with ice as needed and add the mixed cocktail.

FRUITY COCKTAIL WITH POMEGRANATE AND MINT

Ingredients for 4 drinks:

1 pomegranate
400 ml orange juice
Juice of 1 lime
12 cl vodka
12 cl Cointreau
600 ml cold mineral water with carbonic acid
Ice cream
Fresh mint

Preparation:

1. Remove the seeds from the pomegranate and squeeze out the juice.

2. Now mix the orange juice, the fresh lime juice, the vodka and the Cointreau and pour into the glasses halfway.

3. Add a few fresh mint leaves. Then add the pomegranate juice and the seeds to the glasses.

BLUE SWIMMING POOL COCKTAIL

Ingredients for 1 jar:
4 cl white rum
2 cl vodka
1 cl Blue Curacao orange liqueur
2 cl coconut cream
1 cl sweet cream
4 cl pineapple juice
Ice cream
1 pineapple slice
1 cocktail cherry

Preparation:
1. Fill a shaker with all of the ingredients except the orange liqueur.

2. Add some ice and shake everything thoroughly.

3. Add some more ice to the glass and fill it up with the cocktail. Finally, add the Blue Curacao for a nice colour.

4. Decorate the drink as desired with a cocktail cherry and a fresh pineapple slice.

YELLOW SLUSHIE COCKTAIL

Ingredients for 1 jar:

100 g passion fruit juice in ice cubes
150 g frozen mango
50 g Licor 43
100 g passion fruit nectar

Preparation:

1. First, freeze passion fruit juice in an ice cube tray.

2. Now put all the ingredients in a blender. Instead of Licor 43 you can also use white rum and vanilla.

3. Pour the contents from the blender into a glass and decorate the finished cocktail with fresh fruit of your choice.

PINK LADY COCKTAIL

Ingredients for 1 jar:
8 ice cubes
60 ml raspberry vodka
10 ml grenadine
20 ml fresh lemon juice
20 ml cranberry juice
Tonic water
Fresh raspberries to garnish

Preparation:

1. First pour the ice cubes into a tall glass.

2. Add the vodka, grenadine, lemon juice and cranberry juice. Then stir briefly and infuse with the tonic water.

3. Serve the cocktail immediately and garnish with a few fresh raspberries.

HEAVENLY MALIBU SUNSET COCKTAIL

Ingredients for 2 drinks:

¼ cup Malibu rum
½ cup pineapple juice
2 cl grenadine
Cherries for garnish
Pineapple chunks for garnish
Ice cream

Preparation:

1. First, fill both glasses with ice.

2. Pour the pineapple juice and rum over the ice cubes.

3. Slowly add the grenadine to the rim of the glasses.

4. Finally garnish the finished cocktails with cherries and pineapple.

PINK COCONUT COCKTAIL

Ingredients for 6 drinks:

1 kg strawberries
2 cans of coconut milk (400 ml)
240 ml vodka
120 ml coconut syrup
2 tbsp white sugar syrup
4 tbsp grated coconut
About 20 ice cubes

Preparation:

1. Wash the fresh strawberries. Leave some for decoration.

2. Put the coconut milk, vodka, syrup and fresh strawberries in a blender and puree until very fine.

3. Now pour the sugar syrup and the coconut flakes onto a flat plate. Place the rims of the cocktail glasses first in the syrup and then in the coconut flakes, so that a nice coconut rim is created on top.

4. Fill each glass with a few ice cubes, add the drink and decorate each glass with the remaining fresh strawberries.

SUMMER WATERMELON COCKTAIL

Ingredients for 2 drinks:

500 g frozen watermelon cubes without seeds
Juice of 1 lime
6 leaves of fresh mint
40 ml gin

Preparation:

1. Cut open a watermelon and gradually remove the seeds.

2. Cut into cubes of about 2 cm and freeze for a few hours.

3. Put the frozen melon in a blender with the mint and puree until very finely.

4. Add the gin and the fresh lime juice and stir. Sweeten a little with syrup to taste.

5. Put everything back in the freezer until it is slightly frozen. Then pour into glasses and garnish with mint.

PURPLE CAIPIRINHA

Ingredients for 1 jar:
1 lime
2 tbsp sugar
1 squeeze of fresh lime juice
6 cl Livo-Livo
1 handful of ice
Fresh lime slices for decoration

Preparation:
1. Cut the lime into eight pieces. Put in a glass together with the cane sugar.

2. Add the fresh lime juice and mix everything together.

3. Now add crushed ice.

4. Fill up the drink with Livo- Livo and mix everything again.

5. Decorate the finished cocktail with fresh lime slices.

BERRY CARDAMOM BRAMBLE

Ingredients for 2 drinks:

6 cl lemon juice
2 cl cardamom syrup
3 cl blackberry liqueur
12 cl gin
Blackberries for decoration
50 g sugar
50 ml water
3 cardamom pods
Ice cubes or crushed ice
Cocktail Shaker

Preparation:

1. First, prepare a delicious cardamom syrup. To do this, break open the capsules. Put the capsules with sugar and water in a pot and simmer over high heat for about 10 minutes. Then drain the syrup through a sieve, collect it and let it get cold.

2. Now add the lemon juice, blackberry liqueur, gin and syrup to the shaker. Fill up with enough ice cubes and mix vigorously. After that, a layer of ice should form on the shaker.

3. Fill the glasses with ice cubes and pour the finished cocktail through a sieve into the glasses. If desired, you can put the fresh blackberries on skewers to decorate the cocktail.

CREAMY MILK COCKTAIL WITH RUM AND HONEY

Ingredients for 1 jar:
200 ml hot milk
1 egg yolk
2 cl white rum
1 tbsp honey
1 pinch of nutmeg

Preparation:
1. First heat the milk in a saucepan until it steams slightly.

2. Add honey to the pot until it dissolves.

3. Beat the egg yolks with a mixer until foamy and add to the milk.

4. Pour the warm drink into a cup. Finally, add the rum and dust with a little grated nutmeg.

SPICY GINGER GIN COCKTAIL

Ingredients for 2 drinks:

For the ginger syrup:
150 g fresh chopped ginger root
200 g sugar
360 ml water

For the cocktail:
75 ml fresh lemon juice
75 ml ginger syrup
45 ml gin
70 g ice cubes
150 ml beer

Preparation:

1. First, put the lemon juice, syrup, gin and ice cubes in a container with a lid. Then shake for about 15 seconds or, if you prefer, put it in a good blender or cocktail shaker.

2. Pour the cocktail into a large glass. Add some more ice if desired and add the beer. Stir again and serve immediately fresh.

DREAM EGGNOG

Ingredients for 8 drinks:

1 bottle of egg liqueur (approx. 0.75 L)
½ L white wine (preferably sweet)
½ L orange juice
1 sachet of vanilla sugar
1 package of cream

Preparation:

1. Put the eggnog, white wine and orange juice in a pot and heat everything.

2. Add the vanilla sugar and mix thoroughly.

3. Whip the cream in a bowl with a hand mixer until stiff. You can also sweeten it a little bit if you like.

4. Pour the punch into the glasses and cover with the whipped cream. If desired, you can dust the cream with a little cinnamon or sugar.

EXOTIC BLUE SPARKLING WINE COCKTAIL

Ingredients for 1 jar:

1 tbsp orange juice
1 tbsp sugar
5 tbsp crushed ice
30 ml Blue Curacao
100 ml iced sparkling wine
20 ml white rum
10 ml brandy
30 ml lemon juice
½ a strawberry

Preparation:

1. Pour the orange juice into a large bowl and dip the rim of the cocktail glass into it. Then rotate the rim of the glass in sugar.

2. Use a blender or a shaker and pour in the ice and other ingredients. Then pour everything into the glass and serve garnished with half a strawberry.

Cocktails without alcohol

COLOURFUL RAINBOW COCKTAIL

Ingredients for 2 drinks:
200 ml cold mineral water with plenty of carbonic acid
1 pinch of blue food colouring
400 ml orange-mango juice
60 ml grenadine
2 skewers
Optional: gummy bears

Preparation:
1. Colour the mineral water with the food colouring.

2. Pour the orange-mango juice into two cocktail glasses.

3. Add the grenadine via a teaspoon at the edge of the glass. Then create different colours in the cocktail - like a rainbow.

4. Now pour the blue water into the glass in the same way with a teaspoon so that the colour changes once again.

5. Put gummy bears on skewers if you like and creatively decorate the jar.

DELICIOUS IPANEMA

Ingredients for 4 drinks:
2 untreated limes
4 tbsp cane sugar
8 cl passion fruit juice
24 cl ginger ale
Crushed ice

Preparation:
1. First wash the lime and cut into thin slices.

2. Now distribute the columns in the glasses and mash them a little, so that fresh juice is formed.

3. Add about a tablespoon of sugar to each glass, then stir the two together.

4. Fill the glasses with crushed ice and add 2 cl passion fruit juice to each glass. Stir properly.

5. Finally, infuse the glasses with ginger ale. If desired, garnish the cocktails and serve immediately.

REFRESHING NOJITO (MOJITO WITHOUT ALCOHOL)

Ingredients for 4 drinks:
1 bunch of fresh mint
2 untreated limes
4 tbsp brown sugar
Crushed ice
500 ml ginger ale

Preparation:
1. Wash the mint and limes. Let dry and pluck the mint leaves from the stems. Cut the limes into wedges.

2. Distribute the mint evenly among the glasses and crush them a little. Then add the limes and crush them as well.

3. Pour a tbsp of brown sugar into each glass and then fill up with ginger ale. Garnish the glasses with fresh mint and serve immediately.

INVIGORATING HUGO

Ingredients for 4 drinks:

350 ml ginger ale
70 ml elderflower syrup
Juice of 2 limes
1 organic lime
1 organic lemon
3 fresh sprigs of mint
400 ml cold mineral water
Some ice cubes

Preparation:

1. First mix the ginger ale, the syrup and the fresh lime juice. Then add the fresh sprigs of mint and fill up with the cold mineral water.

2. Now wash the organic lime hot and pat dry. Cut it into slices and halve it. Leave four slices and add the other slices to the remaining ingredients.

3. Fill four large glasses halfway with ice cubes or crushed ice and pour in the non-alcoholic Hugo. Garnish each glass with a slice of lime.

SPARKLING MOJITO WITH FRESH MANGO

Ingredients for 2 drinks:

1 ripe mango
1 fresh lime
½ bunch of fresh mint
0,5 L cold mineral water
Some ice cubes

Preparation:

1. First peel the ripe mango and carefully cut the flesh from the core.

2. Halve the lime and squeeze out the fresh juice.

3. Finely puree the pulp of the mango, the juice of the lime and about 12 leaves of mint with a stand mixer - you can also use a stick.

4 Now divide the mixture between two glasses and pour about 200 ml of cold mineral water into each.

5. Finally, add a few ice cubes to each glass. Garnish the cocktails with a fresh sprig of mint, if desired.

AUTUMN ROSEHIP COCKTAIL

Ingredients for 4 drinks:
4 bags of rose hip tea
2 tbsp vanilla syrup
2 tbsp hazelnut syrup
4 tsp lemon juice
60 cl ginger ale
4 vanilla beans

Preparation:
1. First boil 400 ml in a kettle and pour it over the tea bags. Let it steep for about 7 minutes. Then remove the tea bags and let the tea cool.

2. Mix the vanilla syrup with the hazelnut syrup. Add the lemon juice and the tea.

3. It is best to use large glasses (about 0.3 L). Fill them with ice cubes and pour the finished cocktail evenly into them. Top up each glass with a little ginger ale.

4. Decorate the cocktail with whole vanilla beans.

TROPICAL COCKTAIL WITH FRESH PINEAPPLE

Ingredients for 2 drinks:

1 pineapple
3 stalks of fresh mint
200 ml fresh or bought orange juice
400 ml mango-passion fruit juice
200 ml pineapple juice

Preparation:

1. First cut off the ends of the pineapple. Then peel and cut into quarters. Remove the stalk of the fruit and cut it into small pieces.

2. Now wash the mint, dab dry and put the leaves together with the pineapple on skewers.

3. Mix the juices together and fill the glasses with ice cubes. Decorate the finished cocktail with pineapple mint skewers.

WOODRUFF COCKTAIL FOR CHILDREN

Ingredients for 4 drinks:
4 tbsp woodruff syrup
0,8 L cold mineral water
0,8 L cold apple juice
Some crushed ice
Effervescent powder in different colours

Preparation:
1. In a large bottle, pour in the mineral water and then add the syrup.

2. Fill a saucer with water and put the powders on different, individual saucers.

3. Hold the rims of the glasses in water and then press into the different colours to create beautiful rims.

4. Fill the glasses halfway with crushed ice. Now pour 150 ml apple juice over it and fill up with the woodruff mineral water mixture. Serve the cocktails with colourful straws.

FRUITY MULTI COLADA

Ingredients for 2 - 4 drinks:

1 pomegranate
3 untreated limes
1 baby pineapple
750 ml vitamin juice
160 ml coconut milk

Preparation:

1. Halve the pomegranate and remove the seeds with a spoon.

2. Wash a lime in hot water, let dry and cut into 8 slices.

3. Peel the pineapple and cut lengthwise into quarters. Make sure that you carefully cut the leaves. Remove the stalk of the fruit.

4. Cut the remaining limes in half.

5. Now add the juice of one lime, the vitamin juice and the coconut milk into a shaker and mix thoroughly.

6. Then divide 4 tbsp of pomegranate seeds and 4 lime slices between 2 glasses and top up with the drink. Depending on the size of the glasses, you can repeat this process with two more glasses.

7. Decorate the glasses with the sliced pineapple.

MANGO COCKTAIL WITH ELDERBERRY

Ingredients for 1 jar:

100 g mango puree
2 tbsp elderflower syrup
½ tsp cumin seeds
100 g sugar
50 ml apple cider vinegar
Cold mineral water
Some ice cubes

Preparation:

1. Cut 100 g of mango from the fruit and put it in a blender or puree it with a stick.

2. Put the puree in a pot with the other ingredients, except the water and the ice cubes.

3. Bring to a boil and then simmer for about 10 minutes until the sugar has dissolved. The end result is a syrup.

4. Now mix about 2 - 3 tbsp of syrup with the mineral water and the ice cubes.

SWEET MANGO GINGER COCKTAIL

Ingredients for 6 drinks:

1 ripe mango
2 tbsp elderflower syrup
1 tbsp sugar
5 cm ginger bulb
Some ice cubes
Cold mineral water

Preparation:

1. Cut out small balls from the mango with a small spoon or a melon cutter.

2. Peel the ginger and cut it into very fine strips.

3. Fill approx. 1 L of water with the elderflower syrup and the sugar into glasses.

4. Arrange with the mango and ginger nicely. Finally, fill the glasses with mineral water and ice cubes.

COLORED COCKTAIL WITH KIWI

Ingredients for 2 drinks:

2 fresh kiwis
3 tbsp orange juice
3 tbsp instant oatmeal
2 fresh peaches
150 g cherries from the jar

Preparation:

1. First peel the kiwis and cut them into small pieces. Then puree together with orange juice and with 1 tbsp of instant oatmeal. Put the mixture into 2 large glasses.

2. Skin the peaches and chop them. Puree them with 1 tbsp of oatmeal. Now add the mixture to the kiwi mixture.

3. Mash the cherries with oatmeal and put on top of the peaches, so that there are three nice layers. Serve immediately.

CHAI BUBBLE TEA LATTE

Ingredients for 1 jar:
2 packets of chai tea
Some cinnamon
A little almond syrup
Soy milk
Tapioca beads

Preparation:
1. First, mix the soy milk with the chai tea.

2. Add a little cinnamon and almond syrup.

3. Add the tapioca pearls and enjoy the drink.

BOOSTER COCKTAIL WITH ROSEHIP

Ingredients for 1 jar:
200 ml cooled rose hip tea
200 ml cherry juice
Juice of ½ a lemon
A little zest of an untreated lemon
1 tsp apple syrup

Preparation:
1. First boil 200 ml of water and add a few tea bags with rosehip flavour. Add the apple syrup so that it dissolves well. Then let it brew and wait until the tea becomes cold.

2. Now put all the ingredients in a shaker and shake everything thoroughly.

3. Finally, pour the finished cocktail into glasses, add ice cubes, and decorate them with fresh fruit.

DELICIOUS BERRY COCKTAIL

Ingredients for 4 drinks:
350 g berry mixture
1 apple
1 pear
1 banana
0,8 L whey
80 g honey

Preparation:

1. First, wash all the berries. Set aside some beautiful berries for decoration. Put these berries on skewers and put them aside, covered.

2. Quarter the banana and cut the apple and pear into smaller pieces.

3. Now put all the fruits in the blender. Then add the whey and honey. Pour the cocktail through a sieve into cocktail glasses.

4. Garnish with the berry skewers and serve with a straw.

HIGH PROTEIN SMOOTHIE COCKTAIL

Ingredients for 2 drinks:

200 g fresh pineapple
150 g low fat curd
150 g yogurt (0.1% fat)
100 ml light coconut milk
10 g coconut flakes
1 fresh lemon
Some ice to taste

Preparation:

1. Peel the pineapple and cut off about 200 g. Cut into small pieces.

2. Put the pieces with a little lemon juice in a blender. Puree briefly and then add the other ingredients.

3. Pour the finished High Protein Smoothie Cocktail into two large glasses and add ice if desired.

BLUEBERRY BANANA COCKTAIL

Ingredients for 2 drinks:

2 very ripe bananas
350 g blueberries
20 cl milk
2 scoops of vanilla ice cream
20 g brown sugar
Some fresh lemon juice

Preparation:

1. First, put all the ingredients, except for the ice cream, in a blender and puree everything finely.

2. Pour the cocktail into two large glasses and add a scoop of ice to each.

3. Garnish the drinks with a few blueberries and serve with a spoon.

GREEN SMOOTHIE COCKTAIL

Ingredients for 1 jar:
1 cup spinach or kale (preferably frozen)
2 cups of different fruits
1 cup water
1 cup orange juice
1 cup almond milk
Spices such as cinnamon or turmeric to taste

Preparation:
1. It is best to use a stand mixer.

2. Put the liquid ingredients in the blender first and then add the spinach and the various fruits.

3. Add spices to taste and then mix everything very finely.

4. Pour into a large glass and add some more ice if desired.

SIMPLE STRAWBERRY COCKTAIL

Ingredients for 1 jar:
Strawberries as desired
1 lemon
Cold mineral water
Some ice cubes

Preparation:
1. Squeeze half of the lemon and pour the juice directly into a glass.

2. Add a few ice cubes if desired.

3. Cut the rest of the lemon into small pieces and add them to the glass.

4. Now chop the strawberries and add them. Squeeze out the juice a little with a stick.

5. Fill up with the cold mineral water. Garnish the rim of the glass with a strawberry.

DELICIOUS STRAWBERRY COCKTAIL WITH TANGERINE

Ingredients for 1 jar:

1 lemon
A handful of strawberries
2 tangerines
Rosemary syrup, depending on the desired sweetness
Fresh mint
Some ice
Cold water with or without carbonic acid

Preparation:

1. First put the strawberries and the tangerines in a stand mixer and process them to a puree.

2. Fill some ice in a glass and add the puree.

3. Fill the glass with water. Then add a little syrup for sweetness.

4. Now add a squeeze of fresh lemon.

5. The glass can be decorated with fresh mint, if desired.

AROMATIC HUGO PUNCH WITH STRAWBERRIES

Ingredients for 1 punch bowl:

500 g strawberries
100 ml elderberry drink
4 tbsp fresh lime juice
2 limes
10 sprigs of fresh mint
0,5 L cold water with carbonic acid
1 bottle of lemonade in the flavour "apple- elderflower"

For the ice cubes:
½ bottle of lemonade in the flavour "apple elderflower"
½ bottle of lemonade in the flavour "apple-rhubarb"

Preparation:

1. Fill the two lemonades into ice cube moulds. Place in the freezer until frozen.

2. Wash the strawberries and cut them into small cubes.

3. Mix the cubes with the elderberry drink and lime juice. Then put in the refrigerator for 30 minutes and leave to infuse.

4. Cut the two limes into fine slices. Then place the lime slices and the fresh mint in a large container.

5. Now fill the container with cold mineral water and lemonade. This also works with dry sparkling wine, if alcohol is desired.

6. Before serving, add a few of the homemade ice cubes to the punch.

HAWAIIAN LAVA FLOW COCKTAIL

Ingredients for 1 jar:
4 - 5 fresh strawberries
6 cl pineapple juice
6 cl cream
A dash of coconut syrup
Some crushed ice

Preparation:
1. First wash the strawberries and remove the leaves. Then puree with a hand blender. For frozen strawberries, add a little vanilla sugar.

2. Fill a glass one-third full with the strawberry puree.

3. Now add crushed ice, pineapple juice, cream and coconut syrup to a shaker and shake vigorously. Shake until the cream is frothy.

4. Pour the cream from the shaker on top of the strawberry puree.

5. Mix the cream and the puree from the bottom to the top, so that a nice pattern is formed.

6. If desired, stick a strawberry on the edge for decoration.

APPLE COCKTAIL WITH CRANBERRY JUICE

Ingredients for 2 drinks:
50 g fresh raspberries
75 ml elderflower syrup
200 ml cranberry juice
250 ml apple juice
Some ice cubes
1 fresh lime

Preparation:
1. Mash the raspberries with a stick or fork.

2. Add the apple juice, elderflower syrup and cranberry juice to a shaker. Also add about one-third of the raspberry puree. Shake thoroughly for a few seconds.

3. Now add ice cubes and the remaining puree to two tall glasses. Mix everything with the contents of the shaker. Then decorate both glasses with a slice of lime.

HAPPY COCKTAIL WITH PASSION FRUIT

Ingredients for 1 jar:

200 ml cold non-alcoholic beer
100 ml cold passion fruit juice
1 - 2 tsp cold lemon juice or lime juice
Some crushed ice
2 cl lemon juice
Grenadine

Preparation:

1. Fill a glass with the beer, passion fruit juice and lime juice. Mix everything with a spoon. Then add the crushed ice.

2. Let some syrup - depending on the desired sweetness - run into the glass at the rim.

3. Garnish the cocktail with fresh lemon slices and serve immediately.

REFRESHING SODA COCKTAIL FOR SUMMER

Ingredients for 1 jar:
Juice of ½ a lime
A few slices of lime
Some almond syrup
Some grenadine syrup
Mineral water for refilling
1 fresh sprig of rosemary
Pomegranate seeds
A few large ice cubes

Preparation:
1. Squeeze the juice of half a lime.

2. Finely slice the rest of the lime.

3. Prepare a glass with a few large ice cubes.

4. Add the lime juice and stick a sprig of rosemary.

5. Now add the pomegranate seeds to the glass and pour in cold mineral water.

6. Add the syrup according to the desired sweetness.

7. Finally, decorate the refreshing drink with fresh lime slices.

SWEET COCKTAIL WITH LIME

Ingredients for 1 jar:

10 - 12 fresh mint leaves
Juice from 1 lime
1 tbsp sugar
12 cl cold mineral water
1 fresh slice of lemon or lime

Preparation:

1. Cut one or more slices of a lime and put them into a glass.

2. Add fresh mint leaves and crush the lime slices a little.

3. Squeeze the juice from the lime and add it.

4. Now add the sugar - a little more if you like.

5. Fill the drink with mineral water and enjoy immediately.

FRUITY MANGO LASSI COCKTAIL

Ingredients for 1 jar:

250 g natural yoghurt (1.5 % fat)
150 ml milk
1 ripe mango
1 tsp lemon juice
1 tsp rose water
A little sugar to taste
Some ice cream as desired
1 sprig of fresh mint for decoration

Preparation:

1. Peel the mango and cut it into small cubes.

2. Put the small cubes in a blender.

3. Add the other ingredients and mix everything very finely.

4. If desired, add some ice to the glass and pour in the cocktail. Garnish with some fresh mint if desired.

PINK BLUEBERRY LEMONADE COCKTAIL

Ingredients for 1 large pot:

1 cup water
1 cup sugar
1 cup lemon juice
1 cup blueberry juice
2 tsp of the zest of an untreated lemon
8 cups crushed ice
Several lemon slices

Preparation:

1. Take a shaker and put in all the ingredients, except for the lemon slices.

2. Shake everything vigorously for several seconds.

3. Pour the drink into a large jug or other container and place a few lemon slices inside. Add crushed ice to taste and serve the delicious drink immediately.

THIRST QUENCHING CRODINO GINGER TONIC

Ingredients for 1 jar:

4 cl ginger syrup
2 cl fresh lime juice
100 ml orange juice
100 ml Crodino
100 ml tonic water
2 sprigs of fresh mint
2 lime slices to garnish
Some crushed ice

Preparation:

1. First, put the ginger syrup, lime juice and orange juice in a shaker and mix well.

2. Add the Crodino and stir once briefly.

3. Fill two large glasses with crushed ice and divide the mixture between the glasses.

4. Pour 50 ml tonic water into both glasses and stir briefly.

5. Serve garnished with a sprig of fresh mint and a slice of lime.

MANGO COCKTAIL WITH FRESH MINT

Ingredients for 2 drinks:

¼ mango
8 fresh mint leaves
1/3 lime
3 tbsp brown sugar
6 ice cubes
Cold mineral water

Preparation:

1. Cut the mango into small pieces and put them in a blender. Puree the fruit to a fine pulp.

2. Now put the puree, the mineral water and the sugar in a shaker and shake everything well.

3. Pour the liquid into two glasses.

4. Cut the lime into small pieces and add them.

5. Add a few ice cubes if desired and enjoy.

COLOURFUL FRUIT PUNCH

Ingredients for 1 jar:

3 L sparkling water
2 oranges
1 apple
Frozen raspberries
Some ice cubes

Preparation:

1. First cut the oranges into rings and the apple into pieces.

2. Now pour the sparkling water into a large container and add the cut fruit with the frozen raspberries.

3. Add some more ice if you like.

4. Let the punch stand for a few hours until the water has turned a little pink.

COCONUT YOGURT COCKTAIL

Ingredients for 1 jar:

1 cup sweet natural yoghurt
½ cup coconut milk
2 tbsp coconut powder

Preparation:

1. Put all the ingredients in a shaker and shake well.

2. Pour into a suitable glass and garnish with some coconut powder if desired.

3. Depending on the consistency, the cocktail is better enjoyed with a spoon.

NEW YEAR'S EVE COCKTAIL WITH STRAWBERRY JUICE

Ingredients for 1 jar:

2 cl mango juice
4 cl passion fruit juice
4 cl orange juice
3 cl strawberry juice
3 ice cubes
1 ½ cl coconut syrup
1 slice of lemon

Preparation:

1. First put all ingredients including the ice cubes into a shaker. Shake everything thoroughly - preferably for 1 minute.

2. Pour the cocktail into a suitable glass.

3. Decorate the cocktail with a slice of lemon and, if desired, a tinsel flag.

APPLE CHERRY TONIC

Ingredients for 1 jar:

2 cl tonic water
1 cl apple juice
2 cl sour cherry nectar
1 squeeze of lime
2 sprigs of fresh mint

Preparation:

1. Fill a shaker with the cherry nectar. Then add a few ice cubes and mint and shake for about 10 seconds.

2. Pour into a large glass. Fill it with tonic water, apple juice and a squeeze of lime.

3. Finally, add a little mint to the glass for decoration.

GAUDY PRIMAVERA

Ingredients for 1 jar:

1 cl lemon juice
4 cl orange juice
4 cl passion fruit juice
4 cl grapefruit juice
2 cl grenadine
2 cocktail cherries
1 orange slice
Ice or crushed ice

Preparation:

1. Mix the grapefruit juice, orange juice and lemon juice. Then add the grenadine and passion fruit juice and mix everything again in a shaker.

2. Mix in some additional ice or crushed ice.

3. Now pour a few ice cubes into a glass and add the mixed cocktail.

4. Garnish the Primavera with a drinking straw, a fresh orange slice and cocktail cherries.

DELICIOUS PEAR COCKTAIL

Ingredients for 1 jar:

For the rosemary syrup:
100 g granulated sugar
100 ml water
2 sprigs of rosemary

For the cocktail:
3 cl pear juice
1 cl rosemary syrup
8 cl tonic water
1 pear
Some cinnamon bark
Star Anise
Fresh thyme

Preparation:

1. First prepare a delicious rosemary syrup. Put all the ingredients for the syrup in a pot and bring to a boil.

2. The sugar should have dissolved completely. Then pull the pot aside and let the syrup cool.

3. Remove the rosemary sprigs and pour the homemade syrup through a coffee filter. Add few ice cubes to a glass.

4. Now add the rosemary syrup and the pear juice and mix everything together. Add the tonic water.

5. Wash the pear and cut it into slices. Put one slice in the glass.

6. Serve with cinnamon bark, star anise and a freshly plucked thyme leaf.

VITAMIN COCKTAIL WITH SEA BUCKTHORN

Ingredients for 1 jar:

50 ml sea buckthorn juice
200 ml pear juice
Juice of ½ an untreated lemon
A little lemon zest
1 tbsp vanilla sugar
1 pinch or ½ tsp cinnamon to taste
1 pear
Some ice

Preparation:

1. First cut the pear into small pieces and put them on a skewer.

2. Pour some ice into a large glass.

3. Now put all the other ingredients in a blender and mix well.

4. Pour the finished cocktail into the glass and serve garnished with the fruit skewer.

BORA BORA COCKTAIL

Ingredients for 1 jar:
4 cl coconut cream
6 cl pineapple juice
4 cl passion fruit juice
Grenadine
Some crushed ice
Pineapple slices

Preparation:
1. Fill a glass with crushed ice.

2. Put all the ingredients, except the grenadine, in a shaker and mix vigorously.

3. Pour the mixed cocktail into the glass and then slowly pour in the grenadine for a nice colour.

4. Decorate the glass with a few pineapple slices.

FRUITY AND CREAMY GIN COCKTAIL

Ingredients for 1 jar:

100 g raspberries
2 tsp cane sugar
10 cl squeezed lemon juice
30 cl lemonade
Some ice cubes
Fresh mint leaves for decoration

Preparation:

1. First put a few ice cubes in a large glass.

2. Add the sugar.

3. Fill the glass with lemonade and squeeze fresh lemon juice. Pour this into the glass.

4. Finally, decorate the drink with fresh mint leaves. Enjoy immediately, cold.

RASPBERRY PUNCH WITH FRESH ROSEMARY

Ingredients for 4 drinks:

250 g raspberries
2 stalks of rosemary
200 ml raspberry juice
4 tsp fresh lemon juice
Ice cubes or crushed ice
600 ml mineral water

Preparation:

1. First wash the fresh raspberries and carefully dry them. Wash the fresh rosemary as well.

2. Divide 200 g of raspberries between 4 glasses and crush them to make the raspberry juice.

3. Now add the rosemary stems to the glasses and pour everything in with the fresh raspberry juice. Then add a teaspoon of fresh lemon juice. Stir everything carefully and fill up with ice. Finally, add the mineral water and enjoy immediately, cold.

EXOTIC SWIMMING POOL

Ingredients for 1 jar:
2 cl Blue Curacao (non-alcoholic)
2 cl coconut syrup
2 cl cream
14 cl pineapple juice

Preparation:
1. Place all ingredients in a cocktail shaker or other blender. Alternatively, use a container with a lid.

2. Mix thoroughly for about 15 seconds. Then pour into a glass and decorate as desired.

INVIGORATING COCKTAIL WITH COFFEE

Ingredients for 1 jar:

Double espresso (approx. 50 ml)
1 tsp brown sugar
3 lemon zests
200 ml apple juice
Some ice cubes

Preparation:

1. Pour the apple juice into a glass with ice cubes, if desired.

2. Prepare the espresso.

3. Pour the finished espresso into a cocktail shaker or blender. Then add the sugar and mix properly together with the lemon zest in the shaker. Finally, add the coffee to the glass.

BITTERSWEET COCKTAIL WITH MINT

Ingredients for 1 jar:

Double espresso (approx. 50 ml)
2 tsp honey or syrup
5 - 6 sprigs of fresh mint
Some ice cubes

Preparation:

1. First, prepare a double espresso.

2. Mix the espresso with the mint and the honey or syrup in a cocktail shaker.

3. When everything is well mixed, add the ice cubes and shake well again.

4. Pour the finished cocktail into a suitable glass and decorate with a few fresh mint leaves.

Small tip: If you want the taste to be a little softer, you can add some milk foam.

DARK ENERGY COCKTAIL

Ingredients for 1 jar:

1 espresso (25 - 30 ml)
200 ml cola
Some ice cubes

Preparation:

1. Place ice cubs in a large glass filled with cola.

2. Prepare the espresso and let it cool down a little.

3. Pour everything into the glass and then decorate with a slice of lemon.

DELICIOUS PELICAN COCKTAIL

Ingredients for 1 jar:
2 cl freshly squeezed lemon juice
6 cl freshly squeezed orange juice
8 cl grapefruit juice
2 cl passion fruit juice
1 cocktail cherry for decoration
1 zest of an organic grapefruit for decoration
Shaker
Crushed ice

Preparation:
1. Take a cocktail shaker and pour in the lemon juice, orange juice, grapefruit juice and syrup. Then close the shaker tightly and shake thoroughly for about 15 seconds.

2. Fill a large glass about halfway with ice. Pour the contents of the shaker into the glass.

3. Finally, decorate the delicious cocktail with a cocktail cherry and the grapefruit zest. Serve immediately.

CREAMY APPLE PUNCH WITH CREAM

Ingredients for 1 litre of punch:

1 apple (preferably Granny Smith)
1 L apple juice
5 cloves
1 cinnamon stick
3 anise stars
200 g whipped cream
½ vanilla pod
1 tsp cinnamon
1 tbsp vanilla sugar

Preparation:

1. First wash the apple and cut it into quarters. Remove the seeds and cut into very fine cubes.

2. Put the apple cubes, apple juice, and spices together into a pot. Then heat everything and keep warm on low heat.

3. For the delicious cream, scrape out the vanilla pod. Then beat the pulp together with the cinnamon, vanilla sugar and the liquid cream with a hand mixer until very stiff.

4. Fill the finished punch into glasses and add the wintry cream on top.

ICED COCKTAIL WITH CHERRIES AND PINEAPPLE

Ingredients for 4 glasses:

4 cl grenadine
20 cl cherry juice
4 cl fresh lemon juice
20 cl pineapple juice
Some ice cubes
1 tbsp crushed ice
4 slices of an untreated lime

Preparation:

1. Put all the ingredients together, including the ice cubes, in a shaker and shake vigorously for about 15 seconds.

2. Put the crushed ice into the glasses. Then pour the cocktail through a sieve into the glasses.

3. Finally, garnish the glasses with the fresh lime slices.

DELICIOUS PASSION FRUIT MANGO COCKTAIL

Ingredients for 1 jar:

100 ml cream
200 ml chilled passion fruit mango nectar
50 ml orange juice
Some ice cubes
2 orange slices

Preparation:

1. First, mix the cream with the juices.

2. Pour a few ice cubes into the glass and pour the mixture into it.

3. Garnish with orange slices and enjoy cold.

WHITE BLUEBERRY COCKTAIL

Ingredients for 4 drinks:

11 g white tea blueberry
1 L water
150 ml white grape juice
4 tbsp frozen blueberries
8 fresh sprigs of rosemary
Some ice cubes

Preparation:

1. Pour the tea into a large pot with about 200 ml of hot water. Let it steep for about 2 minutes.

2. Pour the tea through a sieve into another pot filled with ice cubes and fill with 1 L of cold water.

3. Place the frozen blueberries into four different jars along with fresh sprigs of rosemary.

4. Fill the glasses with the tea and enjoy chilled.

FRUITY LEMONADE COCKTAIL WITH POMEGRANATE

Ingredients for 1 jar:

4 tbsp agave syrup
150 ml water
Some chopped fresh ginger
A handful of fresh mint
Crushed ice
200 ml pomegranate juice
100 ml grapefruit juice
Juice of ½ a lime
1 small sip of cinnamon syrup
Pomegranate syrup
A few pomegranate seeds
Mineral water for refilling

Preparation:

1. First, put the agave syrup, water and ginger in a saucepan and bring to a boil. Then remove from the heat and add the fresh mint. Cover the mixture and allow to cool.

2. Pour enough pomegranate seeds into the glass to cover the bottom. Then fill the glass about a third full with ice.

3. Now add the pomegranate juice, the grapefruit juice and the lime juice. Refine the cocktail afterwards with some cinnamon syrup and the cooled syrup from the pot.

4. Fill up with mineral water and decorate with fresh mint and lime slices as desired.

JUICY BANANA COCKTAIL

Ingredients for 1 jar:

10 cl banana juice
10 cl passion fruit juice
3 cl grenadine syrup
Some crushed ice
About 2 ice cubes

Preparation:

1. First pour the banana juice, passion fruit juice and grenadine into a cocktail shaker. Then add the ice cubes and shake everything vigorously.

2. Take a large glass and fill it halfway with crushed ice, followed by the cocktail. Best served with fresh lemon slices and enjoyed immediately, cold.

STRAWBERRY GARDEN COCKTAIL

Ingredients for 1 jar:

50 g fresh or frozen strawberries
5 cl orange juice
1 cl lemon juice
Some ice cubes
Some cane sugar or vanilla sugar of your choice
Strawberries for decoration

Preparation:

1. First wash the fresh strawberries, remove the green and cut them in half. Then put them in a shaker with two ice cubes and shake everything thoroughly.

2. Add the contents of the shaker, the orange juice, the fresh lemon juice and, if desired, the sugar together with two ice cubes in the shaker and mix thoroughly.

3. Pour the finished cocktail into a large glass and add a few ice cubes or crushed ice if desired.

4. Give free rein to your creativity when decorating, e.g. you can cut the strawberries into small pieces and put them on skewers or stick the strawberries on the rim of the glass.

VALENTINE'S DAY COCKTAIL WITH ELDERBERRY

Ingredients for 1 jar:

1 small chilled bottle of San Bitter
100 ml chilled mineral water
1 lime
Some chilled elderflower syrup
Ice cubes to taste
Straw (with heart motif as desired)
Heart confetti

Preparation:

1. First pour the chilled bottle of San Bitter into a large wine glass. Then add the chilled mineral water.

2. Cut 2 - 3 slices of lime. Squeeze the rest of the lime and add it to the glass.

3. Add a little elderflower syrup - the syrup is very sweet, so taste carefully!

4. Finally, you can add a few ice cubes or crushed ice. You can use a nice straw for decoration and spread heart confetti around the glasses.

POMEGRANATE COCKTAIL

Ingredients for 1 jar:

For the syrup:
500 g fresh or frozen pomegranate seeds
200 g fresh or frozen raspberries
100 ml water
2 tbsp erythritol
1 ½ tsp starch plus 2 tbsp water

For the cocktail:
50 ml syrup
200 ml mineral water
1 large ice cube
1 tsp fresh lemon juice
A few raspberries
A sprig of fresh rosemary
Some pink pepper

Preparation:

1. First put the pomegranate seeds, the raspberries, the water and the chosen sweetener in a pot.
2. Let it simmer for a few minutes on medium heat. Remove the pot from the heat and then puree with a stick.
3. Pour the pureed mixture through a sieve and collect the liquid. Return the collected liquid to the pot and bring to a boil over medium heat.
4. Mix the starch with the water and stir this mixture into the pot. Bring to a boil briefly until the liquid thickens.
5. Pour the syrup into a sealable container for storage.
6. Now pour a few ice cubes into a glass. Then pour in the syrup and lemon juice.
7. Pour mineral water into the glass until it is full.
8. Afterwards, the delicious drink can be garnished with raspberries, a sprig of rosemary and pink pepper.

INVIGORATING PEACH ROSÉ

Ingredients for 4 drinks:

1 peach
600 ml non-alcoholic Mumm Rosé Dry
100 ml water
100 g sugar
½ a lemon
Some chopped peach for decoration
Ice cubes

Preparation:

1. First wash the peaches. Then cut them in half, remove the pit and cut into small pieces.

2. Bring the water and sugar together in a saucepan and heat to a boil, and then reduce the heat slightly.

3. Add the peach cubes to the pot and simmer a little longer.

4. Now cut the lemon in half and squeeze out the juice. Add it to the pot. Remove the pot from the stove and mash the peaches lightly with a fork.

5. Cover the pot and let everything infuse for another 20 minutes. Then pour into a sieve. If desired, cut another peach into wedges for decoration.

6. Divide the peach syrup from the saucepan between the glasses and top up with the rosé. Decorate as desired and then drink immediately.

REFRESHING WATERMELON GIN TONIC

Ingredients for 2 drinks:
1 slice of watermelon (approx. 1 - 2 cm wide)
40 ml Siegfried Gin (non-alcoholic)
140 ml cold tonic water
1 strand of fresh apple mint

Preparation:
1. First, puree the fresh watermelon. Then distribute through the sieve into the two glasses.

2. Add about 2 tsp of the remaining pulp to each glass.

3. Chill the jars in the refrigerator for about 5 minutes.

4. Use 40 ml of gin and 140 ml of tonic water per glass. Add about 3 ice cubes or some crushed ice per glass along with one strand of fresh mint.

CREAMY ORANGE PINEAPPLE COCKTAIL

Ingredients for 1 jar:

Some ice cubes
8 cl orange juice
8 cl pineapple juice
2 cl grenadine
2 cl cream

Preparation:

1. Put all the ingredients in a cocktail shaker with a few ice cubes. Shake everything vigorously.

2. Pour ice cubes or some crushed ice into a glass and pour the mixed liquid through a sieve into the glass. Then garnish with fresh orange slices or pineapple chunks.

DELICIOUS ORANGE PUNCH

Ingredients for 1 L punch:

1 L orange juice
2 cinnamon sticks
1 clove
1 star anise
200 ml cream
1 sachet of vanilla sugar
1 sachet of cream stiffener
1 untreated orange

Preparation:

1. First, put the orange juice in a pot. Season the orange juice with cinnamon, cloves and star anise. Heat the whole thing slightly.

2. In the meantime, prepare the cream. To do this, whip the cream together with the vanilla sugar, the cream stiffener and the grated orange until stiff.

3. Pour the punch into glasses and cover with the creamy whipped cream. The punch is best served nice and warm.

© William Rooley

2023

ISBN: 9798857161029

1st edition

Contact: Markus Mägerle/ Am Kreisgraben 17/ 93104 Riekofen/ Germany

Printed in Great Britain
by Amazon